TURNING FROM...
TURNING TO...

MY TURNING POINT

QueenDeborah

ISBN 978-1-63874-292-0 (paperback)
ISBN 978-1-68517-480-4 (hardcover)
ISBN 978-1-63874-293-7 (digital)

Christian Faith Publishing, Inc.
832 Park Avenue
Meadville, PA 16335
www.christianfaithpublishing.com

Printed in the United States of America

I am dedicating this book, first into GOD'S hands to reach all HE desires it to reach.

I am dedicating this book to my past self that I am truly forgiven and washed in and by the BLOOD of JESUS!

I am dedicating this book to my present self because GOD has called me to HIS KINGDOM for such as a time as this!

I am dedicating this book to my future self what is to come is GREATER and better than what has been!

Finally, I dedicate this book to all that have had, will have, and have reached a TURNING POINT! TURN your all to GOD; HE will not lead you wrong!

CONTENTS

INTRODUCTION

This writing was inspired by the Spirit of GOD to encourage others the importance and understanding of TURNING FROM a present state and TURNING TO a place that may be sustained only by the GRACE, MERCY, and LOVE OF GOD! GOD moved me to write this book. I started on March 17, 2021, and completed it by March 19, 2021. When I started writing, it was exactly one month from my birthday and the exact date that GOD brought me to my TURNING POINT! Not knowing one month ago that GOD was going to use this experience to make me an author and birth my PURPOSE! What seemed to be the worst of times, GOD TURNED it to be the BEST of times! GOD TURNED IT and gave me MY TURNING POINT! How exciting!

And be not conformed to this world: but be ye transformed by the renewing of your mind. (ROMANS 12:2 KJV)

TURNING FROM and TURNING TO something usually happens after a situation, place, or thing that seems so insurmountable occurs and the only option is to TURN. Where does that decision of TURNING take place? It is in the MIND!

TURNING POINTS are linked to a place of exhaustion, devastation, depression, betrayal, hurt, pain, loss, argument, and or catastrophe, to the point where one would ask, what happened? It plays such a pivotal moment in the mind that there is no question or error but to come to grips that something must change and/TURN!

CHAPTER 1

MY TURNING POINT

When I got to this place, I was at a devastating and hurtful place and time! I have been raised in the Apostolic Pentecostal faith my entire life.

> *Then Peter said unto them, Repent, and be baptized every one of you in the name of Jesus Christ for the remission of sins ye shall receive the gift of the Holy Ghost.* (ACTS 2:38 KJV)

I am baptized in Jesus Christ's name and filled with the Holy Ghost. I am saved and sustained by GOD's GRACE.

> *For by grace ye are saved through faith and not of yourselves: it is the gift of GOD.* (EPHESIANS 2:8 KJV)

GRACE is GOD's gift to us because HE knew we are not perfect but that we are fragile, frail, and without HIM, we would fail!

> *But the free gift is of many offenses unto justification.* (ROMANS 5:16 KJV)

Prior to the outbreak of the COVID-19 pandemic, I was engaged but called off the engagement for information I discovered that was not beneficial to me. Then within a month (wow, the enemy of our souls moves quickly to destroy us), I met a charming guy whom at this time we will call Charles. Charles was everything I thought and believed I desired and wanted in a man!

I have eleven brothers, dated, been engaged, married, and divorced, and at this time, I am single by choice. I believed I knew what I (emphasize *I*) wanted at this time in my life. This guy, Charles, was educated and adventurous. We had great laughs, had a blast together, enjoyed traveling, had a lot of similarities in our careers, life experiences; and I pictured us being the exact replication of each other. Or so I thought! The most important and missing ingredient was having JESUS CHRIST as the centered focus! Yes, I am going to tell on myself! I knew better!

When I met Charles, the Spirit of GOD said, *Haste makes waste!* Well, again I (emphasize *I*) wanted this relationship even though I was being warned by GOD. Within nine months, seven out of those nine, we disagreed once a month; and I thought, because we had so many similarities and interests, we would work through it!

How many know "what works through it" means? One minute, you could be up and down. In love one minute and at odds or hate the next. I thought, if we genuinely loved someone, we would do what? We would work through it!

One of my work-through-it strategies is that of writing out a T-chart that narrows down all the pros and cons of the relationship, and then if I really feel stuck, I would write out the likes and dislikes! This strategy—chess game, the manipulation of the mind—is all a game to see if we can change someone, convince them to change, or it is a justified behavior of the mundane!

There were several times I mentioned to Charles that I did not like how he made me feel. I am very accomplished and pleased with all the things GOD has helped me to achieve. I am a huge perfection-ist and a high achiever! But when you are total opposites with an individual, if it is in one area or many, that area of difference(s) and what does not mesh will always stand out!

> *You will forget what a person said or did, but you will never forget how they made you feel.*
> *(MAYA ANGELOU)*

In this process and journey of living the life I thought I desired and what was best for me at that time, I being a HOLY GHOST-filled believer, GOD gave me a conscious and it would tug at me. The Spirit of GOD would say, *You know he is not saved, you know you have been saved for almost thirty years, and you know better!* Yes, I did know better! Again, this is what I wanted! *At least from all that was falsely being portrayed,* or so I thought!

> *When you know better, do better. (MAYA ANGELOU)*

Who else in the Bible has been pointed out to have the "I" problem or trouble?

> *For thou hast said in thine heart, I will ascend into heaven. I will exalt my throne above the stars of God: I will sit also upon the mount of the congregation, in the sides of the north: I will ascend above the heights of the clouds; I will be like the most High. Yet thou shalt be brought down to hell, to the sides of the pit.*
> *(ISAIAH 14:15 KJV)*

We see in the verses about the devil whose name is Lucifer, one of God's angels at that time, who dared thought he could be like God! He had the "I" trouble! Anytime one's life is centered on "I this," "I that," "I choose," "I decided," yeah, one is in danger of pride and hell's fire.

> *Pride goeth before destruction and an haughty spirit before a fall. (PROVERBS 16:18 KJV)*

> *THE AMERICAN HERITAGE COLLEGE Dictionary defines PRIDE as "a pleasure or satisfaction taken in an achievement, a possession, or an association; or an arrogant or disdainful conduct or treatment, or haughtiness."*

PRIDE is extremely dangerous in the sight of GOD. I believe, anytime that we step over the small voice of GOD, the WORD of GOD, the counsel of the wise (i.e., parents, siblings, counselors, even our kids [they have intuition too]), we are operating in a spirit of PRIDE.

> *GOD opposes the proud, but gives grace to the humble. (JAMES 4:6 AMP)*

GOD loves us enough to warn us in one or many ways or another, and we choose to stay in the spirit of PRIDE! I wanted what I wanted when I wanted it! And that is why we get hurt, brokenhearted, disappointed in the end, because we did not listen at the beginning!

WOW! Can anyone be honest and lift both hands, both feet, or—forget that—STAND UP and say, "Yes, that's me" or "Yes, I have been there!"

During my time with Charles, GOD ALMIGHTY did everything but stand directly in front of me to let me know this is NOT where HE designed me to be! May I stop and repent and say this was not the first time! Every guy I (I trouble) dared to launch out and date outside GOD's

will and faith, GOD warned me about aforetime! A lot of those relationships could have been over in a day, week, or month if only I had chosen
to listen and not fallen for the same foolery to be in a relationship!

Why do we persist in a damning, deadly, and hellish behavior, knowing, if JESUS CHRIST would allow us to die or split the sky
and the Rapture took place, our eternity would be sealed forever!
Wow! Why does GOD love us so much to tolerate such egregious and
opposing behaviors?

> *Because sentence against an evil work is not
> executed speedily, therefore the heart of the
> sons of men is fully set in them to do evil.
> (ECCLESIASTES 8:11 KJV)*

Wow again! GOD, forgive us! I pray GOD would help me to
always have a repentant heart before HIM, even while writing this
book. If GOD sentenced us as swiftly as some judges did in their
courtrooms, where would we be?

During this time with Charles, I fell asleep at his house. But while
I slept, I have no consciousness or awareness of this! Charles said I was
asleep but woke up out of my sleep, pointed at him, yelling "JESUS,
JESUS, JESUS, JESUS!" and he stated I said it fast! "JEEEEEESSSSUUUSSSS,
JEEEESSSSUS!" He stated it scared him, so he ran! (Again, I was not
conscious of this!) I told this to my family and hairdresser, and they
stated, "That is POWERFUL!" How the Spirit of GOD in me rose out
of me without any awareness or without me being conscious. Used
my body to rebuke devils and demons that desired to entrap me and
destroy the ANOINTING of GOD in and on me. But GOD stood up in me

and said, "No!" Charles told me what happened. He explained every-thing that transpired! The Spirit and POWER of GOD are POWERFUL!

> *Not by might, not by power, but by my Spirit*
> *saith the LORD. (ZECHARIAH 4:6 KJV)*

Even after Charles expounded to me about this experience that I was not conscious about, it was not enough for me to stop and to consider my ways.

> *Now therefore, thus saith the LORD, of hosts;*
> *Consider your ways. (HAGGAI 1:5 KJV)*

As many of us single women do when we enter a relationship, we are always thinking, hoping, and praying things could work out even when we know a relationship is not befitting for a child of GOD or as a daughter of the KING of KINGS! I recalled to my mind several times what GOD already spoke over this relationship, "Haste makes waste!"

The weird thing is that, in my finite small mind, I was trying to outwit what GOD said! Every month that time lapsed and I was still in the relationship, I was like, "See, GOD, we were still moving forward!" In my sight, I was blinded by things that were not visible to me, but GOD sees all!

> *Let GOD be true and every man a liar.*
> *(ROMANS 3:4 KJV)*

I told my two young adults an epiphany a thought from GOD HIMSELF, one night while watching a movie, "That when you do not know who you are within and operate from that place, you'll com-promise and negotiate without!"

The foolery was on me, NOT GOD! I stayed in this toxic relationship! We had too many disagreements; it even got to a point where a third party was asked to intervene each time—an adage, "Two is company, and three is a crowd!" This relationship was becoming very crowded! Yes, it was becoming too much! At this time in my life, I had anxiety and troubles hitting on all sides! Maybe GOD was trying to tell me something!

Now seven months in this relationship that I thought I could work through, I would always ask GOD, "How did I get in this relationship? GOD, how did I get here?" Over and over, I asked GOD this. Have you ever asked GOD or asked yourself this? I thought I had outgrown this place by not dating guys who did not believe or have faith, knowing it would be a waste of time! I recall being in a relationship a couple of years prior and GOD said, "Because I am not a PRIORITY to this man, you're not going to be!" Okay, do not judge me! You have your struggles and issues too!

My former pastor, the late Dr. Bishop Michael Ford Sr., preached a sermon, "Grab your tissues, we all have issues!" So because I am being authentic and transparent, do not frown, look down, and smirk because, if your walls could talk—yeah, we've all got those silent stories! And if you say "Oh no, I do not!" welp, Mr. and Ms. Perfect, ask GOD to take you now from this earth because you are that perfect!

Have no confidence in the flesh.
(PHILIPPIANS 3:3 KJV)

One of my eleven brothers stated, "You wanted a relationship, and this is what you allowed!"

Happy is he that condemneth not himself in that
thing which he alloweth. (ROMANS 14:22 KJV)

When we get ourselves involved in anything that we want and allow, we've got to stop blaming other people! I never blamed Charles! I decided to entertain this relationship. I knew we were not on the same page spiritually, and I knew it never would have worked! Never! I had to apologize to myself for living this fantasy of a lie! It was a fantasy like any other that had to be exposed and come to an end. A lot of times, we want a Cinderella ending with Prince Charming, but when GOD pulls the rug, it turns out to be the ugliest of all! I had to admit that I did it; GOD pulled the rug so I would quit it and knew that I had to SNAP out of it!

We see all over the world it is hard for people to be honest with GOD, themselves, and let alone others! So many people living double lives in which they want their cake, cookies, jelly, and whipped cream too! Why people cannot be honest is because they are manipulators, liars, and downright selfish! Selfish people do not care whom they hurt or how long they try to hide in the dark! But everything in dark must always come to light! The new term for these people is *narcissist*, just self-absorbed!

> *Therefore whatsoever ye have spoken in the darkness shall be heard in the light. (LUKE 12:3 KJV)*

> *For every one that doeth evil hateth the light, neither cometh to the light, lest his deeds should be reproved. (JOHN 3:20 KJV)*

> *Who both will bring to light the hidden things of darkness, and will make manifest the counsels of the hearts. (1 CORINTHIANS 4:5 KJV)*

All right, seven months in this nine-month relationship, GOD spoke to me again in prayer, "You have to let go!" GOD did not say

"I think" or "if I was you," but HE said, "You have to let go!" I stopped praying for a minute, like, GOD, are you serious! I did not want to let go! There it is again, that "I" problem! But because I am not ALL-SEEING and ALL-KNOWING, GOD is, and HE was watching everything that was going on behind closed doors, in the darkness, and the hidden agendas and plans that I was not privy to know, it just behooves us to listen and stop questioning GOD! GOD help us! GOD truly knows, and we've got to let HIM be GOD! GOD our Protector, Security, Shepherd, Father, Friend, Comforter, Compass, Director, our EVERYTHING—and Trust that HE will not steer or lead us wrong!

But guess what? After GOD ALMIGHTY told me, "You have to let go," that was not enough. But Valentine's Day, February 14, 2021, the unbelievable—the unbelievable for me, but NOT for GOD, who already knew what was going on in the dark—happened! Throughout these nine months of our relationship, I had female intuitions—spidey senses or, as some would say, gut feelings. In my journal entry dated January 3, 2021, I wrote something was lying dormant! I did not know what and could not pinpoint it. GOD started bringing things to my mind, like people we crossed paths with in the park (several), behaviors that were abnormal, and so many other things that did not make sense before but made sense now. GOD called this connecting the dots! You know, the game connecting the dots and where, after all the connections are made, a picture appears! Welp, this picture became crystal clear!

First, there was a text message that he brushed off and downplayed. Which I now believe had validity. We stopped by a gas station because my stomach was hurting so bad! Upon my return to the car, he played a voice mail that explained everything! My brothers asked, "Did he intentionally play the voice mail in front of you?" Either yes or GOD always had a perfect timing! How GOD allowed me to get in the car at that moment! Wow! (Yes, *wow* is a significant word for me.)

Charles's response was speechless and priceless at the same time! There was none! It was like a deer in headlights, and I have never seen what a deer in headlights looked like until this moment! I am telling you I was truly at an "OH MY GOD" moment! I am not sure what caused you to have a TURNING POINT, but this definitely was mines!

TURNING FROM...TURNING TO...

My Turning Point

_____
_____
_____
_____
_____
_____
_____
_____
_____
_____
_____
_____
_____
_____
_____
_____
_____
_____
_____
_____
_____
_____
_____
_____
_____
_____
_____
_____

CHAPTER 2

TURNING FROM...TURNING TO...

Turning from self-will to GOD's will!

O LORD, thou hast searched me, and know me. Thou knowest my downsitting and mine uprising, thou understandest my thought afar off. Thou compassest my path and my lying down, and art acquainted with all my ways. For there is not a word in my tongue, but lo, O LORD, thou knowest it altogether. Thou hast beset me behind and before and laid thine hand upon me. Such knowledge is too wonderful for me; it is high, I cannot attain unto it. Whither shall I go from thy spirit? or whither shall I flee from thy presence? If I ascend up into heaven, thou art there: if I make my bed in hell, behold, thou art there. If I take the wings of the morning, and dwell in the uttermost parts of the sea; Even there shall thy hand lead me, and thy right hand shall hold me. If I say, Surely the darkness shall cover me; even the night shall be light about me. Yea, the darkness...and the light are both alike to thee. For thou hast possessed my reins: thou hast covered me in my mother's womb. I will praise thee; for I am fearfully and wonderfully made: marvellous are thy works; and that my soul knoweth right well. My substance was not hid from thee, when I was made in secret, and curiously wrought in the lowest parts of the earth.

Thine eyes did see my substance, yet being unperfect; and in thy book all my members were written, which in continuance were fashioned, when as yet there was none of them. How precious also are thy thoughts unto me, O God! how great is the sum of them! If I should count them, they are more in number than the sand: when I awake, I am still with thee. Surely thou wilt slay the wicked, O God: depart from me therefore, ye bloody men. For they speak against thee wickedly, and thine enemies take thy name in vain. Do not I hate them, O LORD, that hate thee? and am not I grieved with those that rise up against thee? I hate them with perfect hatred: I count them mine enemies. Search me, O God, and know my heart: try me, and know my thoughts: And see if there be any wicked way in me, and lead me in the way everlasting. (PSALMS 139:1–24 KJV)

Yes, the Psalms above speak of GOD; in HIS infinite stature, He so strategically and fearfully made us individually who we are! Verse 21 tells us to hate what GOD hates! This relationship truly brought me to TURNING from SELF-WILL to GOD's WILL!

Growing up, I have heard people say, "Man's extremities are GOD's opportunities!" I would tell GOD, "You know how to reach me!" GOD knew exactly what to do to tear up this relationship that HE did not want to begin, let alone last nine months! But having had two children of my own, I am reminded that nine months is the due date and time for birth! In this instance, it was long enough for GOD to expose and reveal the darkness that only HE could see when I was not around but that He loved me enough for me to find out and to decide! MY TURNING POINT!

When GOD exposed this to my naked eye, it was a fork in the road! I believe it was a fight between both worlds. The devil said, *Deal with this, and die spiritually and naturally!* GOD said, *LET GO and live!* GOD gave me the courage to do what was best for my soul—our soul, who we really are within this body of flesh that is only a piece of dust! I looked in the mirror and told my soul, *I am sorry for putting you through this!* My soul LOVES JESUS!

> **From the end of the earth will I cry unto thee,**
> **when my heart is overwhelmed: lead me to the**
> **rock that is higher than I. (PSALMS 61:2 KJV)**

Who else is higher than I? I do not know about you, but when I was at my lowest so many times in this game called life and when I did not know what to do being at rock bottom, JESUS's LOVE LIFTED ME! When nothing else could help, JESUS's LOVE helped, rescued, delivered, and lifted me! Now I know that this could not be any kind of LOVE; it had to be the LOVE of the Creator! The one who strategically finessed, framed, created, measured, and constructed me in my mother's belly!

In testimony services at church, I heard a lot of people say, "When I did not know what to do, where to turn, and had nowhere to go, I got on my knees and TURNED to GOD." I believe that's exactly where GOD wants us: to TURN to HIM! If we could do everything on our own without acknowledging GOD, we would never have to TURN to HIM! But GOD loves creating and allowing those circumstances when HIS creation must TURN TO HIM!

JESUS CHRIST HIMSELF had the knowledge that HE must be crucified and be disconnected from HIS HEAVENLY FATHER for a moment to bear the iniquities and sins of this wicked world. HE prayed.

> *He went away again the second time, and prayed, saying, O my Father, if this cup may not pass away from me, except I drink it, thy will be done. (MATTHEW 26:42 KJV)*

When we come to a TURNING POINT—TURNING FROM and TURNING TO—it may come with a cost, and usually, that cost is giving up our self-will! It has been stated that 50 percent of marriages end in divorce. Why? From my own marital experiences, whether one or both parties refused to yield and operate in self-will, that will destroy anything!

As a child of fifteen, I believed that this is where I first learned diversity. My mother taught us all to love GOD, get our education; and in her teachings, being humble and selfless was the way! From my mother, having a great relationship with GOD with HIS aiding were birth engineers, computer experts, teachers, entrepreneurs, police officers—yeah, diversity to the umpteenth power! She birthed kids who got their PhD, Master's, Bachelor's, and Associate's, and/ some type of trade!

Even though my mother was married, I was raised in a single-parent home. I called this married but living single! I knew this when I went through this in my marriage. I knew I did not desire to repeat that cycle; I got divorced. GOD blessed me to soar while raising my two young children, whom I call Royals. They have been high achievers in spite of what statistics state about single-parent households.

GOD HIMSELF has guarded and shielded me throughout this game called life! My mother always stated, "Life is a game, and everyone must play on a team, whether you like it or not!"

> *Choose you this day whom ye will serve.*
> *(JOSHUA 24:15 KJV)*

GOD taught me early the importance of loving myself!

> *I will praise thee; for I am fearfully and wonderfully made. (PSALMS 139:14 KJV)*

I had dealt with rejection in life from my family, church, and working environments because of GOD's anointing on my life and how GOD made me! I learned not to be apologetic for being who HE made me to be—authentic, honest, kind, and at times, forward. I am not perfect, but I had to learn not to be less than whom GOD made me and not to play in and feed into people and their insecurities! I am not a person who curses and goes off even when I am ticked off like a firecracker. GOD keeps my tongue; but people will try to bring you down to their level, pull you out of character, and/try to get you to act uncivilized!

I wrote a song when I was a little girl, a young age: "GOD, fill me with your love so that hurts do not penetrate and rejection does not faze me!" I had to learn at a young age not to care or regard what people thought or said about me! I had to! The ways GOD would use me to be a trendsetter to step out and do things others were fearful to do. I COULD NOT CARE!

When I was young, I was very fearful; and I talked to my pastor at that time—the late Dr. Bishop Michael Ford Sr.—and he told me that GOD told him to tell me, "Walk in your deliverance from fear!" So when GOD delivers you from something, He replaces it with something else, and that was GREATER BOLDNESS! I would do anything! I tell my mother to this day, I am so grateful she raised me in church! Because the adventure and BOLDNESS GOD put in me, that is where the enemy has been wanting to destroy me. I have tried sky-diving, kayaking, white-water rafting, and anything of adventure! So when GOD knew the spirit of the devil was using this relationship to pull me away from what I knew better, GOD was like "All no! I have invested too much time with QueenDeborah!"

> *THE AMERICAN HERITAGE COLLEGE Dictionary states that* INVESTMENT *is "a commitment, as of time; a military siege; or a garment or an outer covering."*

Another definition of *investment* is "to surround a place with hostile force"! Wow, GOD is hostile about me!

I have been raised in church all my life; and to have a relationship with ALMIGHTY GOD for almost thirty years, HE was not just going to let me just walk away! When GOD unveiled and uncovered this ungodly, unhealthy, and toxic relationship, I felt GOD was like, "QueenDeborah, I am not letting you go that easily! GOD showed me I am worth fighting for. GOD HIMSELF will fight for me!"

> *If the Son therefore shall make you free, ye shall be free indeed. (JOHN 8:36 KJV)*

On March 14, 2015, GOD thundered to my spirit *LOVING the UNIQUELY YOU!* I hurried and got this name trademarked! I loved the sound of it! After GOD exposed, revealed, and pulled the rug with this relationship, I had to go back to what GOD told me, "*LOVING the UNIQUELY YOU*"! When relationships come to an end, usually that calls for a TURNING POINT and a lot of self-reflection! I had to start loving myself the way GOD taught me, not leaving one relationship and going into another! I had to readmonish and have self-care to love my good, bad, or ugly, sides; my mistakes; and the insecurities I felt with feeling vulnerable.

Other than JESUS CHRIST, can you name anyone who is perfect and without any flaws?

He that is without sin among you, let him first cast a stone. (JOHN 8:7 KJV)

So without JESUS HIMSELF justifying a woman who was caught in the very act of adultery, HIS love lifted her beyond her mistakes.

TURNING FROM...TURNING TO...

My Turning Point

_____

_____

_____

_____

_____

_____

_____

_____

_____

_____

_____

_____

_____

_____

_____

_____

_____

_____

_____

_____

_____

_____

_____

_____

_____

_____

_____

_____

_____

_____

CHAPTER 3

TRUST GOD, YOUR GUT, YOUR HEART, AND PAY ATTENTION TO RED FLAGS

Every TURNING POINT in our lives calls for a new level of TRUST! Who else better to TRUST than GOD? Some people say, to trust in a higher power, focus your energy on something bigger than yourself; but for me, I know GOD ALMIGHTY is real! HE speaks, responds, and at times, HE may be silent! Read (Psalms 115:3–7 KJV).

> *Be still, and know that I am GOD.*
> *(PSALM 46:10 KJV)*

When did GOD create Eve?

> *And the LORD GOD caused a deep sleep to fall upon Adam, and he slept: and he took one of his ribs. (GENESIS 2:21 KJV)*

> *For GOD speaketh once, yea twice, yet man perceiveth it not. In a dream vision of the night, when deep sleep falleth upon me, in slumberings upon*

*the bed; Then he openeth the ears of men, and
sealeth their instructions. (Job 33:14–16 KJV)*

Why is it that GOD must speak to us in our sleep? Maybe that
is the only time we are being still and silent! Things that we should
ponder.

*I heard Steve Harvey said, "Intuition GOD
gave to women to protect themselves!"*

This statement is so true, but how many of us women really
allow intuition to save and spare our hearts from heartbreak? One
of my brothers (again, I have eleven brothers) told me, "You gave
Charles too many passes!" Yes, in relationships, we tend to stretch
and extend them much longer than what they needed to be.

*When someone shows you who they are, believe
them. (MAYA ANGELOU)*

Do we really want to believe what we see? As mentioned, before
I was trying to outwit GOD to show HIM GOD, Haste is not making
waste! In the relationship, I even got to a point of calculating weeks
(e.g., we have been together nine months, multiplied by 30 days,
equals 270, and if we had a disagreement, once a week, and on and
on). Welp, you see our human minds would do anything to stay in
a relationship that should have been torn apart the first week, much
less the first month!

When the reality of who Charles was sealed in black and white,
with no shades of gray, and after hearing that voicemail, I said,
"Something does not sound or feel right!" He stated, "If it walks like

a duck and quacks like a duck, then it is a duck! You are darn skippy! Yep, call it for what it is! Out of his own mouth, call it, for what it is!"

Trust in the LORD with all our heart and lean not on our own understanding. (PROVERBS 3:5 KJV)

We give too much time, attention, and energy to a person when we do not pay attention to our intuition, hearts, guts, and the red flags that are presented to us. I am at the point where I can say, "GOD, without You, I cannot do Your will! I cannot be obedient! I cannot do what is right, and without You, I am nothing!"

(JESUS said): for without me ye cannot do nothing. (JOHN 15:5 KJV)

Fellow readers, slow down. Okay, I am going to say that again for myself: slow down! Pay attention to your intuition, heart, gut feelings, and especially the leading of GOD!

Howbeit when he, the Spirit of truth is come, he will guide you into all truth. (JOHN 16:13 KJV)

In our finite small minds, we try to make GOD a liar; when HE says and tells us something, it is exactly what HE says it is!

God is not a man that he should lie. (NUMBERS 23:19 KJV)

Let God be true, but every man a liar. (ROMANS 3:4 KJV)

Which God, that cannot lie. (TITUS 1:2 KJV)

I told myself, at this TURNING POINT in my life, I am not fussing, arguing, and I just want to live, love, and embrace what GOD wants me to be" godly happy! Not only happy but JOYFUL!

Neither be ye sorry; for the joy of the LORD is your strength. (NEHEMIAH 8:10 KJV)

My Turning Point

CHAPTER 4

FORGIVENESS

What is a book about TURNING FROM and TURNING TO, without declaring forgiveness! We've got to repent as a people to GOD! As I am writing this book, I just say, "GOD. forgive us because this world has forgotten GOD and who HE is. and so have GOD's people!

> *If my people who are called by my name shall humble themselves, and pray, and seek my face, and turn from their wicked ways; then will I hear from heaven and will forgive their sin, and will heal their land. (2 CHRONICLES 7:14 KJV)*

> *The wicked shall be turned into hell and all the nations that forget God. (PSALM 9:17 KJV)*

As we are the people of GOD, GOD wants to show off HIS POWER, but HE needs our partnership and agreement!

A lot of times, we say we are waiting on GOD, but truly, GOD is waiting on us! GOD genuinely wants us in healthy and advancing relationships! What is the use of being in a relationship where you are both constantly at odds, your feelings are on an emotional roller coaster, you do not know what direction you are headed, and the relationship seems like it is a game of tug-of-war? What is that?

Can two walk together except they be agreed?
(Amos 3:3 KJV)

To walk with GOD in love and forgiveness, we've got to agree with HIM! Once we have asked for GOD's forgiveness, we need to forgive ourselves!

For all have sinned, and come short of the glory
of God. (Romans 3:23 KJV)

This can be one of the hardest things to do, especially when this flesh and the devil want us to be reminded and accused daily of our sins and shortcomings.

For the accuser of our brethren is cast down:
which accused them before our GOD day and
night. (Revelation 12:10 KJV)

As adults, we believe that we are grown seven times three and we are big and grown enough to do whatever it is we want to do! Because GOD is invisible, we tend to treat GOD extremely poorly, like HE is secondary! I raise my hands! GOD, I am sorry, and with HIS help, REPENT! GOD once said to me, "You see how easy it is to do what you want without considering My feelings?"

GOD has feelings too! I have heard people say "NO, HE does not!" But GOD, who made male and female, why would GOD have feelings?

So God created man in his image...male and
female created he them. (Genesis 1:27 KJV)

Male and female created he them.
(GENESIS 5:2 KJV)

At times, we are our worst and biggest enemy at the same time! We are the judge and jury of our own crucifixion and fate! If we hang ourselves before giving GOD a chance to reach us, we sabotage ourselves! I would always tell GOD throughout this relationship with Charles, "GOD, you know how to reach me!" Forgiving ourselves is the only way we may forgive others!

MADEA, in the movie DIARY OF THE MAD BLACK WOMAN,
says, "You forgive others for yourself, not for them!"

If forgiving others frees ourselves, how much more do we need to unlock the door of the dungeon where many are holding themselves captive!

Forgiving ourselves sets us free to trust, love, take a risk, and lower the walls we build to shield ourselves. Unforgivingness to me sounds like it could look something like this...visualize a solid, fortified concrete castle with a narrow entrance one way in and one way out but shut tight!

A brother offended is harder to be won than a
strong city; and their contentions are like bars
of a castle. (PROVERBS 18:19 KJV)

At times, it feels like it is okay to be angry and not to forgive, but it is only hurting us! Some people are so backed up (forgive this description), so constipated with unforgiveness, they should go and see a specialist, and/worse, people who are naturally constipated must get a colonoscopy bag because, without the toxins leaving their bodies, they can die. Forgive yourself and others to live!

I remember telling a relative that they hurt me with what they said and did. I told them, if there was anything that I might have done that caused them to treat me a certain way, that they forgive me. This person just looked at me with a slighted, cold, and odd grin. No "*Forgive me,*" as well, or "Forgive me if I inadvertently," or even a statement saying "I do not think I did, but forgive me," or "I apologize!" There was nothing! I just hugged this individual, walked on, and said, "Jesus, you see!"

People wonder why things have happened in their life or things have not gone the way they have planned them to go. Maybe it is because they are constipated in more ways than one! One of those reasons being unforgivingness!

I always tell my children I do not like saying I am sorry because that may become a self-fulfilling prophecy inadvertently.

> ***Thou art snared by the words of your mouth.***
> ***(Proverbs 6:2 KJV)***

> ***Death and life are in the power of your tongue.***
> ***(Proverbs 18:21 KJV)***

I taught my children to say to people, "*Oh, my bad,*" "*my apology,*" "*I apologize,*" just anything but "*I am sorry.*" We may be sorry for an act, but the act is an error, not who we are! I guess that leads me to my next question to ask, WHO AM I?

My Turning Point

_____

_____

_____

_____

_____

_____

_____

_____

_____

_____

_____

_____

_____

_____

_____

_____

_____

_____

_____

_____

_____

_____

_____

_____

_____

_____

_____

_____

CHAPTER 5

BUILDING UP OURSELVES (KNOWING WHO WE ARE)

But ye, beloved, building up yourselves on your most holy faith, praying in the Holy Ghost. (JUDE 1:20 KJV)

I am only existing because of the privilege and honor of GOD allowing me to have a relationship with HIM! In 2020, I viewed the question "WHO AM I?" Again, WHO AM I?

But many that are first shall be last; and the last shall be first. (MATTHEW 19:30 KJV)

So the last shall be first, and the first last: for many be called, but few chosen. (MATTHEW 20:16 KJV)

When GOD has called and chosen someone, they are totally under GOD's radar, and the enemy wants them too! Instead of saying

"*WHO AM I?*" say it backward, "*I AM!*" In 2013, GOD taught me the "I AM" factor is what HE called it!

> **And God said unto Moses, I AM THAT I AM: and he said, "Thus shalt thou say unto the children of Israel, I AM hath sent me unto you. (EXODUS 3:14 KJV)**

GOD led me to get a letter out of the alphabet and make three words out of it and speak it over my life!

> **Death and life are in the power of your tongue. (PROVERBS 18:21 KJV)**

My letter is the letter *B*. My words are "*I AM BRAVE*," "*I AM BOLD*," and "*I AM BEAUTIFUL!*" You should try this practice for yourself. Find you a letter, and pronounce life over yourself, and watch how you will view, think, and see yourself in a whole new, positive light! Practice makes perfect! You must be consistent for the progress.

We are not our mistakes or sins, but children of the Most High GOD!

> **Beloved, now are we the sons of God, and it doth not yet appear what we shall be. (1 JOHN 3:2 KJV)**

Some people do not feel like they are somebody until they are with somebody! WRONG! Do everything that makes you an asset to whoever you meet and NEVER a liability! A man should complement you, and it should not be that you are depending on him to just fund you. I observed, a man respects a woman more when he has observed she can hold her own! Unlike the relationship with Charles, GOD knew he was no good for me anyway! So when and if GOD shows you this early, please do not waste valuable time. But it is sad that pain must be our teacher. But declare with me, "This is my TURNING POINT!"

Death and life are in the power of your tongue.
(PROVERBS 18:21 KJV)

When GOD gave me the "I AM" factors in 2013, I started seeing "I AM" statements everywhere! This is how I knew that I was in tune and in line with what GOD was telling me to speak over my life! If this is truly a practice that you truly wish to start, let me help you get started.

I AM A CHILD OF GOD.

I AM A QUEEN/KING.

I AM RESILIENT.

I AM ROYALTY.

I AM BLESSED.

I AM CONFIDENT.

I AM ENOUGH.

I AM COMPLETE IN JESUS.

I AM THE HEAD AND NOT THE TAIL.

I AM CAPABLE.

I AM MORE THAN A CONQUEROR.

I AM STRONG.

I AM A WARRIOR.

I AM LOVED BY GOD! You may go on and on! The "I AM" factor is speaking over your life whatever you need it to be according to the affirmations needed to build yourself up! Build yourself up; speak well of yourself. You will come out of this because there are so many examples in GOD's Word in which HE helped so many before us, and HE has ALL POWER to do it again! GOD knows how to heal and mend the broken hearts!

> *All power is given unto me in heaven and in earth. (MATTHEW 28:18 KJV)*

> *Jesus Christ the same yesterday, and today, and forever. (HEBREWS 13:8 KJV)*

While reading this book, I do not know what brought you to your TURNING POINT, where you realized that you had to TURN FROM and TURN TO! But you know that this TURNING POINT had to take place! It is nothing worse than when GOD allowed a TURNING POINT but, instead of TURNING FROM, you TURNED BACK!

Do NOT TURN BACK to the foolishness, weakly, and beggarly elements.

> *But now, after that ye have known God, or rather are known of God, how turn ye again to the weak and beggarly elements, whereunto ye desire again to be in bondage? (GALATIANS 4:9 KJV)*

As MAYA ANGELOU said, "When you know better, do BETTER!" It is time to do BETTER! Leave all the clowns in the circus! Give them that big red nose, floppy shoes, the bushy hair, the big bow tie, the rigid suspenders, the different striped colors, hats, and makeup to cover who they really are! LET those clowns be clowns, and the joke is on them! *Honk, honk!* GOD, who is light, will always expose darkness when it comes to HIS children! Read your bibles. GOD DOES NOT play all the time! And neither do I!

You can't put a CROWN on a CLOWN and expect a KING. (Michael Baisden)

Until the Lord come, who both will bring to light the hidden things of darkness, and will make manifest the counsels of the hearts. (1 CORINTHIANS 4:5 KJV)

I am a witness that GOD will and has removed all that would distract, block, sabotage, or hinder the DESTINY and PURPOSE HE has ordained for my life! I understand now at MY TURNING POINT—TURNING FROM self-will and TURNING TO GOD's will—I cannot just date anybody, and at this point, I know GOD HIMSELF will not allow me to marry anybody! Exposure caused me to call off two engagements!

Welp, GOD told me that my book does not have to be long, to be strong! This is only the beginning until my next book, (*My Pain Birthed My PURPOSE! I SNAPPED OUT of It!*) already typed in the works; the sequel to this; ***Keep It Movin'!*** I call this my "K.I.M." Positivity goes much further than negativity! Onward, Upward, and Forward! No TURNING BACK!

My Turning Point

ABOUT THE AUTHOR

QueenDeborah is a child, along with fifteen other siblings, and raised by her mother, Irietta! She taught QueenDeborah and her siblings to love GOD and to get her education. QueenDeborah has eleven brothers and three other sisters. Most of her siblings have a PhD, Master's, Bachelor's, Associate's degrees, or degrees in other trades!

QueenDeborah has a Bachelor of Science in Justice Administration and Associate of Arts in Paralegal Studies, both obtained from the University of Louisville. She has a class certification in project management and over twenty years' experience in management.

QueenDeborah was chosen by GOD at the age of thirteen and has ministered as GOD has sent her. She is the CEO of LOVING the UNIQUELY YOU Ministry, where she admonishes others to LOVE and embrace their unique selves and to be reminded that the Rapture of JESUS CHRIST can come any day, whether HE cracks the sky or call people individually.

QueenDeborah is a single mother by choice of two awesome young adults she calls her young ROYALS. Destiny Renee is currently an art major and a senior in college to obtain a Bachelor's degree in fine arts and graphic art design. Darius Lamont is a prestigious drummer who will be attending college this fall of 2021 in jazz music.

QueenDeborah is a high achiever. She has enjoyed skydiving, white-water rafting, kayaking, horseback riding, and anything of healthy adventure that does not go against her morals and standards.

The woman QueenDeborah states she owes GOD all the glory for giving her a mother who gave her to GOD!

QueenDeborah is resilient, and in spite of all that she has grown and gone through, GOD has always seen fit to bring her out on top! "How you doing?" is one of her favorite euphemisms!

QueenDeborah loves serving others! With her ministry group, she has served in shelters and reached out in the community.

QueenDeborah loves education and learning new things! She always tells her mother that giving her to GOD was the best gift because being in church has kept her grounded.

GOD is QueenDeborah's everything, and she believes there are no limits to what GOD can do!

CPSIA information can be obtained
at www.ICGtesting.com
Printed in the USA
JSHW050147030622
26605JS00001B/1